....

To:

....

From:

....

Date:

Shaoey, Love took us in and
everything changed . . .

Stevey Joy, you make everyone you
meet smile. You are truly a *joy*!

Maria, we look forward with
anticipation to the day we SEE
fully the story God entrusted
us with here on earth. We love
you . . . to infinity and beyond . . .

You Were Always in My Heart

A Shaoey & Dot Adoption Story

by Mary Beth & Steven Curtis Chapman

illustrated by Jim Chapman

A Division of Thomas Nelson Publishers

NASHVILLE   DALLAS   MEXICO CITY   RIO DE JANEIRO

Published in Nashville, Tennessee, by Tommy Nelson. Tommy Nelson is a registered trademark of Thomas Nelson, Inc.

Thomas Nelson, Inc., titles may be purchased in bulk for educational, business, fund-raising, or sales promotional use. For information, please e-mail SpecialMarkets@ThomasNelson.com.

Library of Congress Cataloging-in-Publication Data:

Chapman, Mary Beth.
  You were always in my heart : a Shaoey & Dot adoption story / by Mary Beth & Steven Curtis Chapman ; illustrated by Jim Chapman.
     p. cm.
  Summary: An abandoned Chinese baby who has been befriended by a ladybug finds her way to an orphanage where she is eventually adopted by an American family.
  ISBN 978-1-4003-2276-3 (hardback)
[1. Stories in rhyme. 2. Intercountry adoption—Fiction. 3. Adoption—Fiction. 4. China—Fiction. 5. Ladybugs—Fiction.] I. Chapman, Steven. II. Chapman, Jim, 1956- ill. III. Title.
  PZ8.3.C3725You 2013
  [E]—dc23   2012042299

Printed in China

13 14 15 16 17 18 TIMS 6 5 4 3 2 1

Dear Families,

For almost two years, our daughter Emily campaigned for us to adopt a baby girl. At first we resisted the idea, but after spending a lot of time thinking and praying, as crazy as we thought it was, we were inspired to extend our family through the miracle of adoption. On March 16, 2000, we walked out of a hotel room in Changsha, Hunan, China, with our daughter Shaohannah (Shaoey for short, pronounced "SHOW-ee"), and our lives were forever changed. Then, a little over two years later, at the dedication ceremony of our friend's adopted son from China, God spoke to us about adopting again. Within days we began the adoption process and went on to complete the adoption of our seven-month-old, Stevey Joy Ru Chapman, in May 2003.

Adoption is a perfect picture of what God has done for each of us in making us His children through Christ. Psalm 68:5–6 tells us that as the Father to the fatherless, God delights in setting the lonely in families. It has been our experience that the scriptural mandate of caring for orphans, such as the one found in James 1:27, is really a wonderful invitation to experience God in a profound way by being a part of His sovereign plan for His precious children.

Working from these foundational truths, we also founded Show Hope, which exists to enable children living without the love and hope of an earthly family to be adopted into "covenant homes." These families can provide not only the love and support needed for this life, but also provide a child with the knowledge of God's plan for his or her eternal life with a forever family called the Body of Christ.

Steven Curtis Chapman
Mary Beth Chapman
cofounders of Show Hope
www.showhope.org

The day started out just like all days before,
With the sun peeking over the trees.
Dot let out a yawn as she stretched out her wings
And went out for a ride on the breeze.

She stopped on a leaf for a quick bite of breakfast
And sipped on a sweet drop of dew,
When off in the distance she heard a strange sound
That was different from any she knew.

Now being the curious bug that she was,
She had to go investigate,
So she followed the sound right down to the ground,
Where a bundle of rags had been placed.

Dot landed softly on top of the bundle.
Then all of a sudden it wiggled!
She started to fly; then she peeked down inside
And saw something that caused her to giggle!

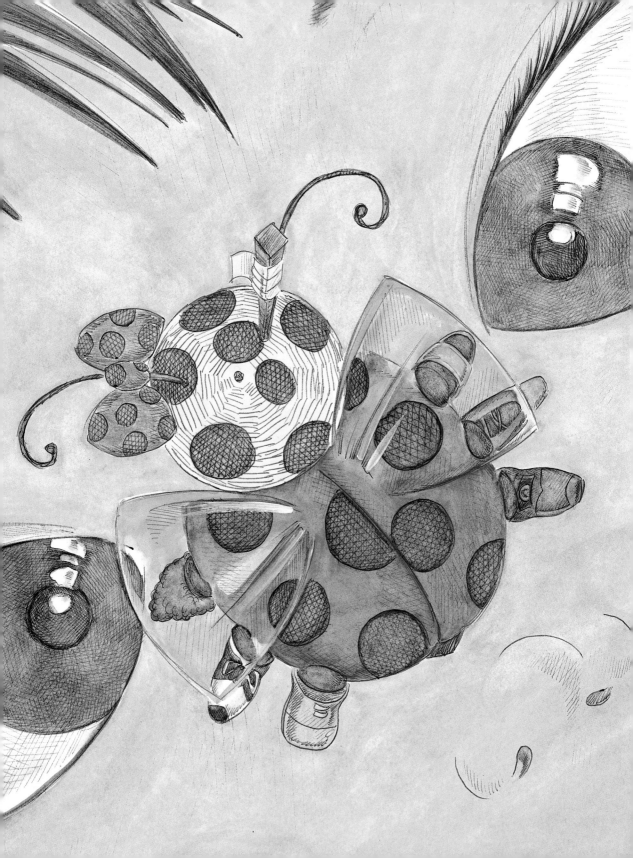

She carefully climbed her way down to a spot
Right between two almond-shaped eyes.
"How cute is this?!" she said to herself.
"What a fabulous little surprise!"

Dot was so taken with this little creature
That she never heard footsteps approaching.
Suddenly she was scooped up with the bundle,
Who was now causing quite a commotion.

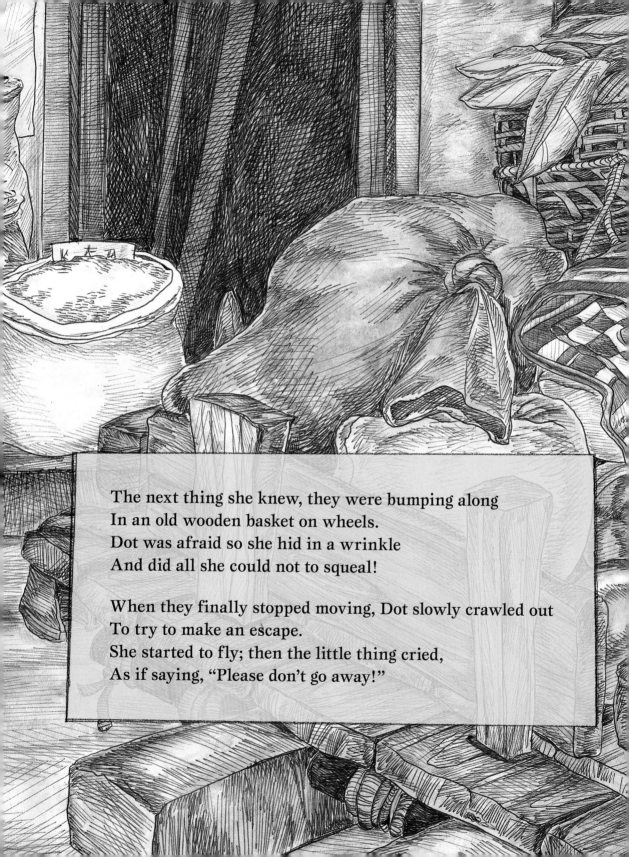

The next thing she knew, they were bumping along
In an old wooden basket on wheels.
Dot was afraid so she hid in a wrinkle
And did all she could not to squeal!

When they finally stopped moving, Dot slowly crawled out
To try to make an escape.
She started to fly; then the little thing cried,
As if saying, "Please don't go away!"

They were in a small room with one little window
That opened to Dot's world outside,
But she just couldn't leave her new little friend,
So she whispered, "I'll stay right by your side."

And so it was there, in that moment of truth,
That Dot's lifetime promise was heard,
'Cause if you know anything about ladybugs,
You know they always keep their word.

Having made her decision to stay with her friend,
Dot said, "Wait here while I go explore."
That's when she discovered the whole room was covered
With bunches of bundles galore.

There must've been dozens of almond-shaped eyes,
All watching as she flew around.
Suddenly Dot realized where they were—
"This is where babies come to be found!"

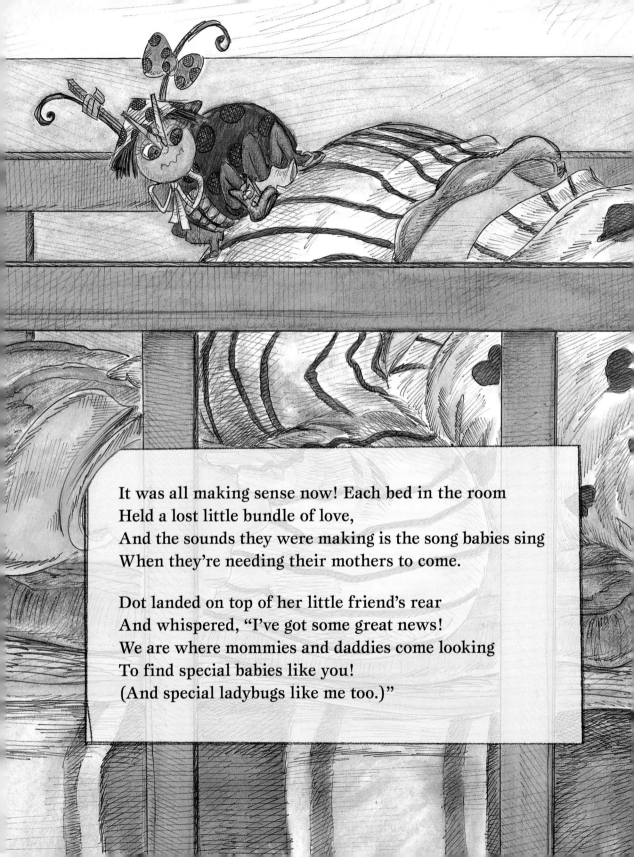

It was all making sense now! Each bed in the room
Held a lost little bundle of love,
And the sounds they were making is the song babies sing
When they're needing their mothers to come.

Dot landed on top of her little friend's rear
And whispered, "I've got some great news!
We are where mommies and daddies come looking
To find special babies like you!
(And special ladybugs like me too.)"

The waiting began, as the days turned to weeks;
Then one morning Dot woke to the sound
Of the ladies in white who took care of the babies
All hustling and bustling around.

The next thing Dot knew, they were covered in bubbles,
Getting scrubbed from antennae to toe.
The ladies were saying, "Your family is waiting.
We'll miss you, but it's your turn to go."

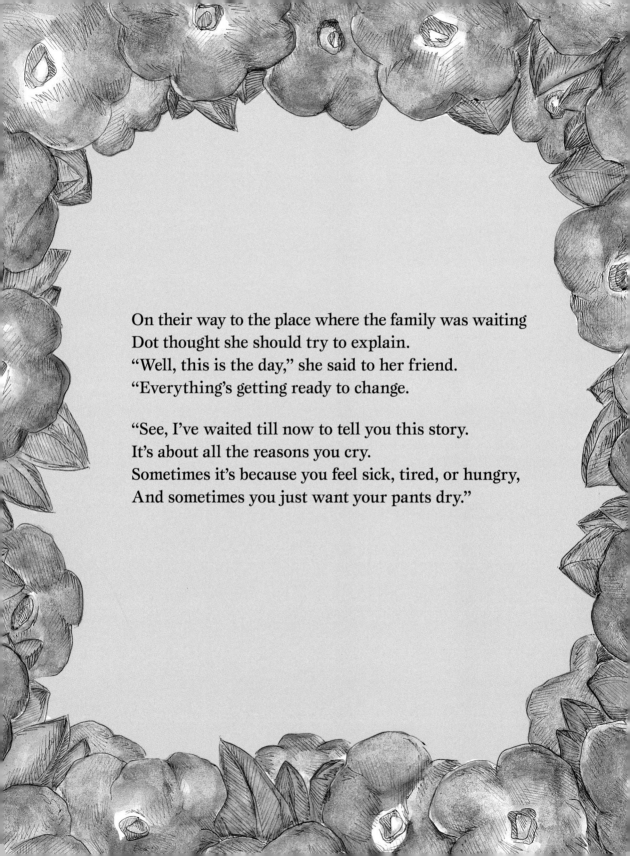

On their way to the place where the family was waiting
Dot thought she should try to explain.
"Well, this is the day," she said to her friend.
"Everything's getting ready to change.

"See, I've waited till now to tell you this story.
It's about all the reasons you cry.
Sometimes it's because you feel sick, tired, or hungry,
And sometimes you just want your pants dry."

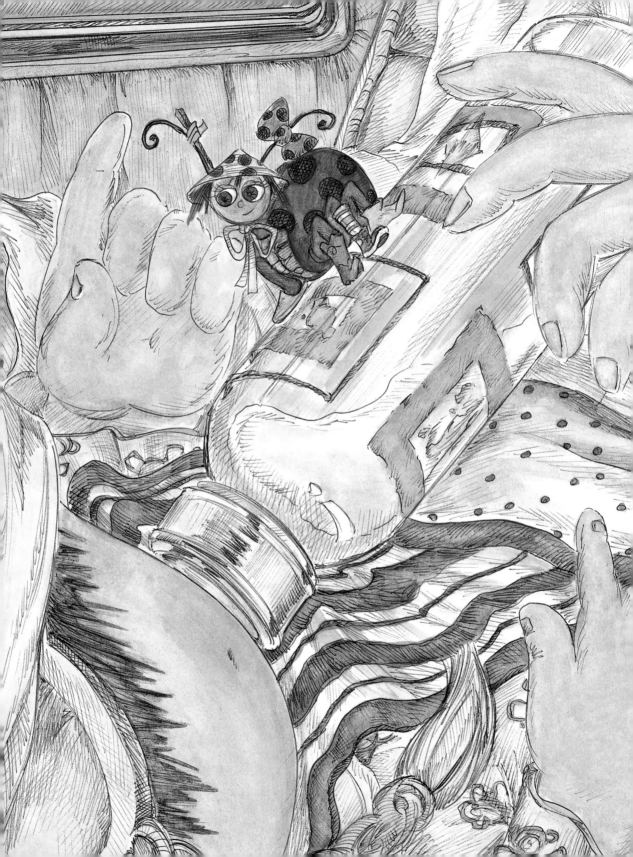

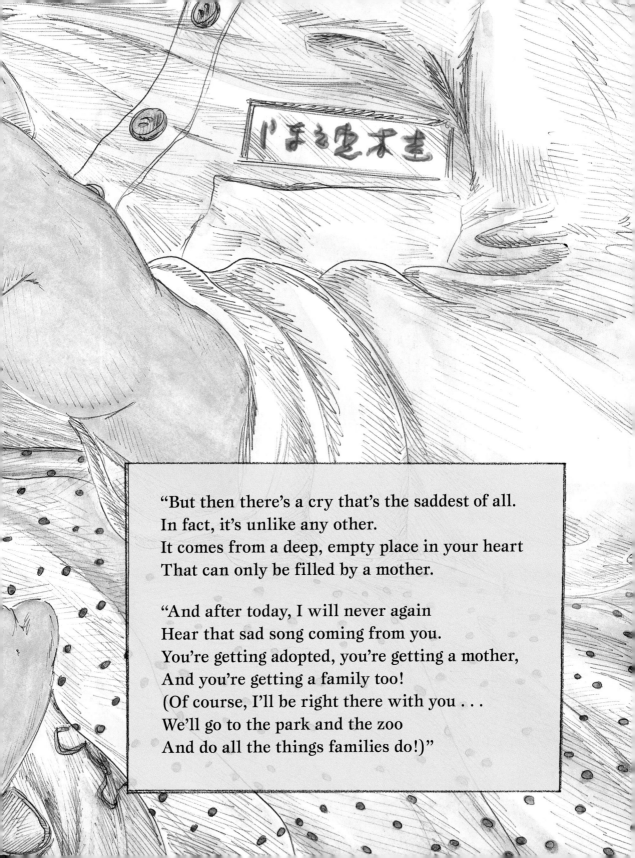

"But then there's a cry that's the saddest of all.
In fact, it's unlike any other.
It comes from a deep, empty place in your heart
That can only be filled by a mother.

"And after today, I will never again
Hear that sad song coming from you.
You're getting adopted, you're getting a mother,
And you're getting a family too!
(Of course, I'll be right there with you . . .
We'll go to the park and the zoo
And do all the things families do!)"

Dot was so caught up in telling her story
That she didn't realize what had happened.
When she looked up, she saw they were all in a room
With ten tearful eyes looking at them.

The cameras all flashed, and everywhere Dot looked,
She saw spots like the ones on her wings.
But what her ears heard was the prettiest song
She'd ever heard anyone sing!

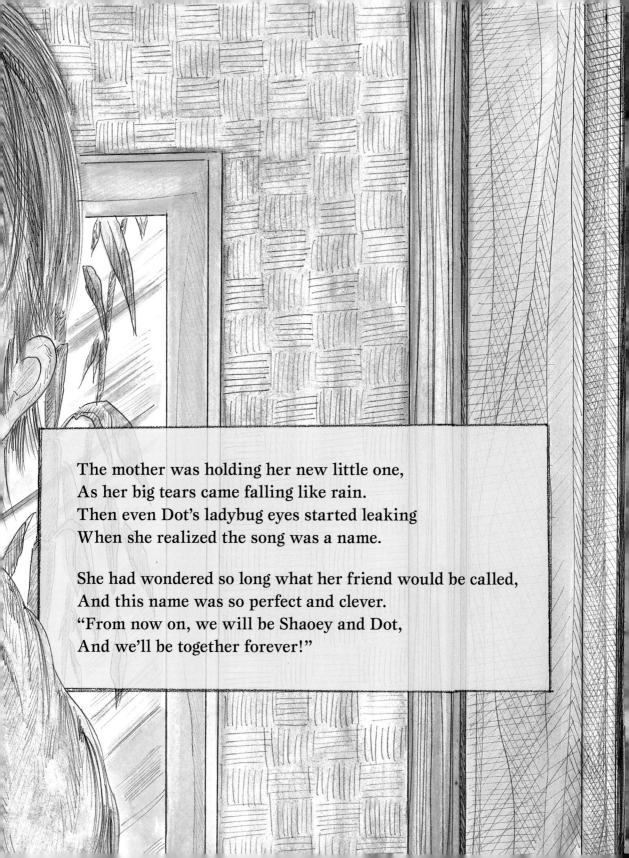

The mother was holding her new little one,
As her big tears came falling like rain.
Then even Dot's ladybug eyes started leaking
When she realized the song was a name.

She had wondered so long what her friend would be called,
And this name was so perfect and clever.
"From now on, we will be Shaoey and Dot,
And we'll be together forever!"

Everything was so strange and exciting and new,
And soon, they were ready to go.
They got in a thing with two humongous wings
That would take them to a place they'd call home!

Mary Beth and **Steven Curtis Chapman** have been married for 28 years and have coauthored three books in the Shaoey and Dot series. Mary Beth is a *New York Times* bestselling author and speaker, and Steven is a beloved songwriter and recording artist who has several certified platinum and gold albums and has won five Grammy® Awards and 57 Dove Awards.

The couple has six children, including three adopted daughters from China, and as founders of Show Hope, they are two of our country's key and leading advocates for orphans in the US and around the world. They have been used by God to lead the charge that has helped thousands of orphans, and at every opportunity, they continue to compel everyone they can to consider the Biblical mandate of adoption and God's heart to care for orphans, our world's most vulnerable children.

StevenCurtisChapman.com MaryBethChapman.com

Jim Chapman, brother to Mary Beth Chapman, is a swim coach and art teacher in middle Tennessee. He and his wife, Yolanda, have seven children, the three youngest coming home through the miracle of adoption.

Show Hope is a ministry that enables individuals and communities to change the world for orphans by not only addressing a child's need for food, shelter, care, and spiritual nourishment, but by also addressing the root issue for an orphan: the lack of a family. Since the formation of the charity in 2003, thousands of orphans have found their forever family with the help of Show Hope adoption assistance grants funded through the generosity of donors, while hundreds are being cared for and given a better chance to be adopted through Show Hope Special Care Centers in China.

ShowHope.org